© Clive Davies 2019
All rights reserved

Reproduction, storage, adaptation or translation, in any form or by any means, of this publication is prohibited without the prior written permission of the publisher. Excerpts may be reproduced for the purpose of research, private study, criticism or review, or by educational institutions solely for educational purposes, without permission, providing full acknowledgement is given.

This publication should only be used be the purchasing organisation or individual. Focus Education does not grant permission for the purchaser to distribute the content of this publication outside their organisation, this includes placing the whole document or parts on social media or internet sites.

First Published in the UK in 2019 by Focus Education (UK) Ltd

Focus Education (UK) Ltd
Publishing
Talking Point Conference & Exhibition Centre
Huddersfield Road
Scouthead
Saddleworth
OL4 4AG

Focus Education (UK) Ltd Reg. No 4507968

ISBN 978-1-911416-21-0

Companies, institutions and other organisations wishing to make bulk purchases of books published by Focus Education should contact their local bookstore or Focus Education direct:

Customer Services, Focus Education, Talking Point Conference & Exhibition Centre,
Huddersfield Road, Scouthead, Saddleworth, OL4 4AG
Tel 01457 821818 Fax 01457 878205

www.focus-education.co.uk
customerservice@focus-education.co.uk
Printed in Great Britain by Focus Education UK Ltd, Scouthead

 focuseducationuk

 focuseducation1

 focus-education-uk-ltd

ABOUT THE AUTHOR

Clive Davies, OBE is one of the founding Directors of Focus working with school both nationally and internationally. He draws on a vast experience, including work as a headteacher, Ofsted inspector, trainer and consultant.

Clive has a wealth of experience working with schools to analyse their current position and supporting leaders to construct purposeful and fit-for-purpose self-evaluation systems which impact on pupil outcomes. Over recent years, Clive has been focusing particularly on the development of an approach to leading and delivering the curriculum which ensures a high degree of engagement for children. This approach to the curriculum is being used in schools across England. He is one of the innovators for the learning challenge curriculum which has gained national acclaim for its success. Clive works in all areas of school improvement and works from early years through the secondary phase.

As a headteacher, Clive's school gained a National Curriculum Award and featured in the TES as one of three schools recognised for its quality practice. Clive has a national and international reputation as an authoritative speaker. He has recently worked in the Middle East, Europe and Japan.

Clive has written a wide range of publications which have become known for their straight forward and useful style; helping school leaders focus on what is most important to making a difference, including the best-selling 'Raising Standards by Setting Targets'. Some of Clive's most recent and best selling publications are:

- Making Good Lessons Outstanding
- Maths Learning Challenge Curriculum: Pre and Post Learning Challenges
- Talk for Success
- Science Learning Challenge Curriculum
- History & Geography Learning Challenge Curriculum
- Leading the EYFS (co-authored with Sarah Quinn)
- Assessing Science and Non Core Subjects: In the new National Curriculum (Years 1 to 6)
- Focus on Maths (co-authored with Helen Rowland)
- Assessing without Levels
- Empowering Learners: A Focus on Learning Behaviours
- Step up to the Challenge Series
- Making Book Scrutiny more Meaningful

Contents

	Pages	Subjects	Pages
Foreword	3	❏ Science	7-19
Introduction	4	❏ Geography	20-24
What do we mean by knowledge-rich?	5	❏ History	25-30
		❏ Art	31-34
What is sticky knowledge?	6	❏ DT	35-38
The school's curriculum is rooted in the solid consensus of the school's leaders about the knowledge and skills that pupils need to take advantage of the opportunities, responsibilities and experiences of later life (Ofsted framework 2019)		❏ Music	39-42
		❏ Computing	43-47
		❏ Physical Education	48-51
		❏ Foreign Language	52-53
		❏ Appendices	54-67

Foreword

Are we doing the Romans or learning about the Romans?

The Emperor   His Army   The Merchants   The Potter The Bather The Farmers

"The truth is that money doesn't make you rich; knowledge does."
Robert Kiyosaki

A well taught knowledge-rich education is potentially the driver for true equality for pupils from different backgrounds. Knowing things, not just recalling the bald facts but deeply understanding them gives pupils confidence. It helps them to discuss a wide range of live topics with their peers, irrespective of their backgrounds'.
Dame Rachel de Souza

Introduction

- One of the main objectives that Ofsted looks for when judging a school's curriculum intent is ensuring sequencing, so knowledge is built over the years.

- The objective expects that:
  *The school's **curriculum is planned and sequenced** so that new knowledge and skills build on what has been taught before, and towards those defined end points.*
  (Ofsted framework – Curriculum intent)

- The following subject specific assessment objectives have therefore been built on this principle. In other words rather than having yearly key assessments for each subject, you can see how an aspect of the subject id built upon by using the main themes such as, locational knowledge in geography or chronology in history.

- In this way, the integrity of the subject is guaranteed with the statements supporting pupils' changes in long-term memory. As a result there is a reduced number of statements so as to achieve this.

- It is also important to remember as outlined by the Education Endowment Foundation that assessing to close to the point of teaching can sometimes be misleading, especially when checking sticky knowledge, that is, learned knowledge that will stay for ever. Therefore we need to recognise that new learning is **fragile** and usually forgotten unless explicit steps are taken over time to revisit and refresh it

- *Teachers should be wary of assuming that pupils have securely learnt material based on* **evidence drawn close to the point of teaching** *(Education Endowment Foundation)*

What do we mean by a 'knowledge-rich' curriculum?

There is an expectation that our curriculum has to be 'knowledge-rich'. What does this mean?
❑ Amanda Spielman (2018) explains that, **'The accumulated wealth of human knowledge, and what we choose to pass on to the next generation through teaching in our schools (the curriculum), must be at the heart of education'**
❑ So what do we need to take into account when planning and assessing our curriculum? Here are some key features to think about:
❑ The curriculum should be a mastery of a body of subject-specific knowledge defined by each school
❑ Skills are the by-product of the knowledge, not its purpose
❑ Schools must decide on the 'invaluable knowledge' that they want their pupils to know as the content of the curriculum
❑ Learning is defined as an alteration in long-term memory. If nothing has altered in long-term memory, nothing has been learned
❑ Progress means knowing more and remembering more
❑ Knowledge is generative or 'sticky'
❑ Vocabulary size is related to academic success, and schooling is crucial for increasing the breadth of pupils' vocabulary

Sticky-knowledge
– What do we mean?

Sticky knowledge is effectively knowledge that will stay with us forever. In other words an alteration has happened to our long-term memory.
We could divide sticky knowledge into two main parts. Firstly, interesting facts that will remain with us forever and secondly, knowledge that individuals need to learn as part of the national curriculum.

Sticky Knowledge

Interesting facts, such as: almost 50% of all plant and animal species can be found in the rainforests

Knowledge required for the **national curriculum: Year 1: Know the names of the four countries that make up the UK**

For the assessment objectives outlined later for geography, history and science, we are referring to the latter – knowledge to learn as part of the national curriculum.

What are the key features of 'knowledge-rich' assessment for science?

Subject	Features

Science	❑ At both key stages the sticky knowledge takes full account of the national curriculum's main characteristics of:
	  ❑ Physics
	  ❑ Chemistry
	  ❑ Biology
	  ❑ Working scientifically

	❑ There are more assessments in science because the national curriculum specifies on a year-by-year basis what has to be taught. In addition, science is a core subject and should have more time devoted to it than non-core subjects
	❑ The working scientifically part does not conform with the knowledge-rich system as it is checking on pupils' ability to, amongst other things, carry out research, ask questions and carry out tests.
	❑ The working scientifically statements should be assessed as an on-going feature of the science lessons, whilst the scientific knowledge should be assessed away from the point of teaching.
	❑ When considering pupils' improvement in science specific vocabulary, see the identified subject specific vocabulary outlined in Focus Education's 'science knowledge mats'.

Year 1

Biology			Chemistry	Physics
Animals, including Humans	**Animals, including Humans**	**Plants**	**Everyday Materials**	**Seasonal Change**
Name common animals *Carnivores, etc*	*Human body and senses*	*Common plants* *Plant structure*	*Properties of materials* *Grouping materials*	*The four seasons* *Seasonal weather*
• Know how to classify a range of animals by amphibian, reptile, mammal, fish and birds • Know and classify animals by what they eat (carnivore, herbivore and omnivore) • Know how to sort by living and non living things	• Know the name of parts of the human body that can be seen	• Know and name a variety of common wild and garden plants • Know and name the petals, stem, leaves and root of a plant • Know and name the roots, trunk, branches and leaves of a tree	• Know the name of the materials an object is made from • Know about the properties of everyday materials	• Name the seasons and know about the type of weather in each season

Year 1

Working Scientifically

- Ask questions such as:
  - Why are flowers different colours?
  - Why do some animals eat meat and others do not?

- Set up a test to see which materials keeps things warmest, know if the test has been successful and can say what has been learned

- Explain to someone what has been learned from an investigation they have been involved with and draw conclusions from the answers to the questions asked

- Measures (within Year 1 mathematical limits) to help find out more about the investigations undertaken

Year 2

Biology			Chemistry	
All living things and their habitats	**Animals, including Humans**	**Plants**	**Everyday Materials**	
• *Alive or dead* • *Habitats* • *Adaptations* • *Food chains*	• *Animal reproduction* • *Healthy living* • *Basic needs*	• *Plant and seed growth* • *Plant reproduction* • *Keeping plants healthy*	• *Identify different materials* • *Name everyday materials* • *Properties of materials*	• *Compare the use of different materials* • *Compare movement on different surfaces*
• Classify things by living, dead or never lived • Know how a specific habitat provides for the basic needs of things living there (plants and animals) • Match living things to their habitat • Name some different sources of food for animals • Know about and explain a simple food chain	• Know the basic stages in a life cycle for animals, (including humans) • Know why exercise, a balanced diet and good hygiene are important for humans	• Know and explain how seeds and bulbs grow into plants • Know what plants need in order to grow and stay healthy (water, light & suitable temperature)	• Know how materials can be changed by squashing, bending, twisting and stretching	• Know why a material might or might not be used for a specific job

Year 2

Working Scientifically

- Ask questions such as:
  - Why do some trees lose their leaves in Autumn and others do not?
  - How long are roots of tall trees?
  - Why do some animals have underground habitats?

- Use equipment such as thermometers and rain gauges to help observe changes to local environment as the year progresses

- Use microscopes to find out more about small creatures and plants

- Know how to set up a fair test and do so when finding out about how seeds grow best

- Classify or group things according to a given criteria, e.g. deciduous and coniferous trees

- Draw conclusions from fair tests and explain what has been found out

- Use measures (within Year 2 mathematical limits) to help find out more about the investigations they are engaged with

Year 3

Biology			Chemistry	Physics	
Animals, including humans	Plants	Plants	Rocks	Forces	Light
• Skeleton and muscles • Nutrition • Exercise and health	• Plant life • Basic structure and functions	• Life cycle • Water transportation	• Fossil formation • Compare and group rocks • Soil	• Different Forces • Magnets	• Reflections • Shadows
• Know about the importance of a nutritious, balanced diet • Know how nutrients, water and oxygen are transported within animals and humans • Know about the skeletal and muscular system of a human	• Know the function of different parts of flowing plants and trees	• Know how water is transported within plants • Know the plant life cycle, especially the importance of flowers	• Compare and group rocks based on their appearance and physical properties, giving reasons • Know how soil is made and how fossils are formed • Know about and explain the difference between sedimentary, metamorphic and igneous rock	• Know about and describe how objects move on different surfaces • Know how a simple pulley works and use to on to lift an object • Know how some forces require contact and some do not, giving examples • Know about and explain how magnets attract and repel Predict whether magnets will attract or repel and give a reason	• Know that dark is the absence of light • Know that light is needed in order to see and is reflected from a surface • Know and demonstrate how a shadow is formed and explain how a shadow changes shape • Know about the danger of direct sunlight and describe how to keep protected

Year 3

Working Scientifically

☐ Ask questions such as: • Why does the moon appear as different shapes in the night sky? • Why do shadows change during the day? • Where does a fossil come from?	☐ Use a thermometer to measure temperature and know there are two main scales used to measure temperature
	☐ Gather and record information using a chart, matrix or tally chart, depending on what is most sensible
☐ Observe at what time of day a shadow is likely to be at its longest and shortest	☐ Group information according to common factors e.g. plants that grow in woodlands or plants that grow in gardens
☐ Observe which type of plants grow in different places e.g. bluebells in woodland, roses in domestic gardens, etc.	☐ Use bar charts and other statistical tables (in line with Year 3 mathematics statistics) to record findings
☐ Use research to find out how reflection can help us see things that are around the corner	☐ Know how to use a key to help understand information presented on a chart
☐ Use research to find out what the main differences are between sedimentary and igneous rocks	☐ Be confident to stand in front of others and explain what has been found out, for example about how the moon changes shape
☐ Test to see which type of soil is most suitable when growing two similar plants	☐ Present findings using written explanations and include diagrams when needed
☐ Test to see if their right hand is as efficient as their left hand	☐ Make sense of findings and draw conclusions which help them to understand more about scientific information
☐ Set up a fair test with different variables e.g. the best conditions for a plant to grow	☐ Amend predictions according to findings
☐ Explain to a partner why a test is a fair one e.g. lifting weights with right and left hand, etc.	☐ Be prepared to change ideas as a result of what has been found out during a scientific enquiry
☐ Measure carefully (taking account of mathematical knowledge up to Year 3) and add to scientific learning	

Year 4

Biology		Chemistry	Physics	
Animals, including humans	**All living things and their habitats**	**States of Matter**	**Electricity**	**Sound**
• Digestive system • Teeth • Food chains	• Grouping living things • Classification keys • Adaptation of living things	• Compare and group materials • Solids, liquids and gases • Changing state • Water cycle	• Uses of electricity • Simple circuits and switches • Conductors and insulators	• How sounds are made • Sound vibrations • Pitch and Volume
• Identify and name the parts of the human digestive system • Know the functions of the organs in the human digestive system • Identify and know the different types of human teeth • Know the functions of different human teeth • Use and construct food chains to identify producers, predators and prey	• Use classification keys to group, identify and name living things • Know how changes to an environment could endanger living things • Group materials based on their state of matter (solid, liquid, gas	• Know the temperature at which materials change state • Know about and explore how some materials can change state • Know the part played by evaporation and condensation in the water cycle	• Identify and name appliances that require electricity to function • Construct a series circuit • Identify and name the components in a series circuit (including cells, wires, bulbs, switches and buzzers) • Predict and test whether a lamp will light within a circuit • Know the function of a switch • Know the difference between a conductor and an insulator; giving examples of each	• Know how sound is made, associating some of them with vibrating • Know how sound travels from a source to our ears • Know the correlation between pitch and the object producing a sound • Know the correlation between the volume of a sound and the strength of the vibrations that produced it • Know what happens to a sound as it travels away from its source

Year 4

Working Scientifically

☐ Ask questions such as: • Why are steam and ice the same thing? • Why is the liver important in the digestive systems? • What do we mean by 'pitch' when it comes to sound?	☐ Gather and record information using a chart, matrix or tally chart, depending on what is most sensible
	☐ Group information according to common factors e.g. materials that make good conductors or insulators
☐ Use research to find out how much time it takes to digest most of our food	☐ Use bar charts and other statistical tables (in line with Year 4 mathematics statistics) to record findings
☐ Use research to find out which materials make effective conductors and insulators of electricity	☐ Present findings using written explanations and include diagrams, when needed
☐ Carry out tests to see, for example, which of two instruments make the highest or lowest sounds and to see if a glass of ice weighs the same as a glass of water	☐ Write up findings using a planning, doing and evaluating process
☐ Set up a fair test with more than one variable e.g. using different materials to cut out sound	☐ Make sense of findings and draw conclusions which helps them understand more about the scientific information that has been learned
☐ Explain to others why a test that has been set up is a fair one e.g. discover how fast ice melts in different temperatures	☐ When making predictions there are plausible reasons as to why they have done so
☐ Measure carefully (taking account of mathematical knowledge up to Year 4) and add to scientific learning	☐ Able to amend predictions according to findings
☐ Use a data logger to check on the time it takes ice to melt to water in different temperatures	☐ Prepared to change ideas as a result of what has been found out during a scientific enquiry
☐ Use a thermometer to measure temperature and know there are two main scales used to measure temperature	

Year 5

Biology		Chemistry	Physics	
All living things and their habitats	**Animals, including humans**	**Properties and changes in materials**	**Forces**	**Earth and Space**
• *Life cycles – plants and animals* • *Reproductive processes* • *Famous naturalists*	• *Changes as humans develop from birth to old age*	• *Compare properties of everyday materials* • *Soluble/ dissolving* • *Reversible and irreversible substances*	• *Gravity* • *Friction* • *Forces and motion of mechanical devices*	• *Movement of the Earth and the planets* • *Movement of the Moon* • *Night and day*
• Know the life cycle of different living things e.g. mammal, amphibian, insect and bird • Know the differences between different life cycles • Know the process of reproduction in plants • Know the process of reproduction in animals	• Create a timeline to indicate stages of growth in humans	• Compare and group materials based on their properties (e.g. hardness, solubility, transparency, conductivity, (electrical & thermal), and response to magnets • Know and explain how a material dissolves to form a solution • Know and show how to recover a substance from a solution • Know and demonstrate how some materials can be separated (e.g. through filtering, sieving and evaporating) • Know and demonstrate that some changes are reversible and some are not • Know how some changes result in the formation of a new material and that this is usually irreversible	• Know what gravity is and its impact on our lives • Identify and know the effect of air and water resistance • Identify and know the effect of friction • Explain how levers, pulleys and gears allow a smaller force to have a greater effect	• Know about and explain the movement of the Earth and other planets relative to the Sun • Know about and explain the movement of the Moon relative to the Earth • Know and demonstrate how night and day are created • Describe the Sun, Earth and Moon (using the term spherical)

© Focus Education (UK) Ltd

Year 5

Working Scientifically

☐	Set up an investigation when it is appropriate e.g. finding out which materials dissolve or not	☐	Able to present information related to scientific enquiries in a range of ways including using IT such as power-point and iMovie
☐	Set up a fair test when needed e.g. which surfaces create most friction?	☐	Use diagrams, as and when necessary, to support writing
☐	Set up an enquiry based investigation e.g. find out what adults / children can do now that they couldn't when a baby	☐	Is evaluative when explaining findings from scientific enquiry
☐	Know what the variables are in a given enquiry and can isolate each one when investigating e.g. finding out how effective parachutes are when made with different materials	☐	Clear about what has been found out from recent enquiry and can relate this to other enquiries, where appropriate
☐	Use all measurements as set out in Year 5 mathematics (measurement), including capacity and mass	☐	Their explanations set out clearly why something has happened and its possible impact on other things
☐	Use other scientific instruments as needed e.g. thermometer, rain gauge, spring scales (for measuring Newtons)	☐	Able to give an example of something focused on when supporting a scientific theory e.g. how much easier it is to lift a heavy object using pulleys
☐	Able to record data and present them in a range of ways including diagrams, labels, classification keys, tables, scatter graphs and bar and line graphs	☐	Keep an on-going record of new scientific words that they have come across for the first time
☐	Make predictions based on information gleaned from investigations	☐	Able to relate causal relationships when, for example, studying life cycles
☐	Create new investigations which take account of what has been learned previously	☐	Frequently carry out research when investigating a scientific principle or theory

Year 6

Biology			Physics	
Animals, including humans	**All living things and their habitats**	**Evolution and Inheritance**	**Electricity**	**Light**
• *The circulatory system* • *Water transportation* • *Impact of exercise on body*	• *Classification of living things and the reasons for it*	• *Identical and non identical off-spring* • *Fossil evidence and evolution* • *Adaptation and evolution*	• *Electrical components* • *Simple circuits* • *Fuses and voltage*	• *How light travels* • *Reflection* • *Ray models of light*
• Identify and name the main parts of the human circulatory system • Know the function of the heart, blood vessels and blood • Know the impact of diet, exercise, drugs and lifestyle on health • Know the ways in which nutrients and water are transported in animals, including humans	• Classify living things into broad groups according to observable characteristics and based on similarities and differences • Know how living things have been classified • Give reasons for classifying plants and animals in a specific way	• Know how the Earth and living things have changed over time • Know how fossils can be used to find out about the past • Know about reproduction and offspring (recognising that offspring normally vary and are not identical to their parents) • Know how animals and plants are adapted to suit their environment • Link adaptation over time to evolution • Know about evolution and can explain what it is	• Compare and give reasons for why components work and do not work in a circuit • Draw circuit diagrams using correct symbols • Know how the number and voltage of cells in a circuit links to the brightness of a lamp or the volume of a buzzer	• Know how light travels • Know and demonstrate how we see objects • Know why shadows have the same shape as the object that casts them • Know how simple optical instruments work e.g. periscope, telescope, binoculars, mirror, magnifying glass etc.

Year 6

Working Scientifically

☐ Know which type of investigation is needed to suit particular scientific enquiry e.g. looking at the relationship between pulse and exercise	☐ Use a range of written methods to report findings, including focusing on the planning, doing and evaluating phases
☐ Set up a fair test when needed e.g. does light travel in straight lines?	☐ Clear about what has been found out from their enquiry and can relate this to others in class
☐ Know how to set up an enquiry based investigation e.g. what is the relationship between oxygen and blood?	☐ Explanations set out clearly why something has happened and its possible impact on other things
☐ Know what the variables are in a given enquiry and can isolate each one when investigating	☐ Aware of the need to support conclusions with evidence
☐ Justify which variable has been isolated in scientific investigation	☐ Keep an on-going record of new scientific words that they have come across for the first time and use these regularly in future scientific write ups
☐ Use all measurements as set out in Year 6 mathematics (measurement), including capacity, mass, ratio and proportion	☐ Use diagrams, as and when necessary, to support writing and be confident enough to present findings orally in front of the class
☐ Able to record data and present them in a range of ways including diagrams, labels, classification keys, tables, scatter graphs and bar and line graphs	☐ Able to give an example of something they have focused on when supporting a scientific theory e.g. classifying vertebrate and invertebrate creatures or why certain creatures choose their unique habitats
☐ Make accurate predictions based on information gleaned from their investigations and create new investigations as a result	☐ Frequently carry out research when investigating a scientific principle or theory
☐ Able to present information related to scientific enquiries in a range of ways including using IT such as power-point, animoto and iMovie	

What are the key features of 'knowledge-rich' assessment for geography?

Subject	Features
Geography	❑ At both key stages the sticky knowledge takes full account of the national curriculum's main characteristics of: ❑ Locational knowledge ❑ Place knowledge ❑ Human and Physical geography ❑ Geographical skills and fieldwork
	❑ There are relatively few assessment statements as these knowledge statements should be what pupils retain for ever. In other words, this knowledge is within their long-term memory and will be retained.
	❑ There is a difference between knowledge which will be retained close to the point of teaching and that which will be retained for ever.
	❑ In effect, sticky knowledge refers to the long-term memory and should not be assessed too close to the point of teaching.
	❑ When considering pupils' improvement in subject specific vocabulary, see the identified geographical specific vocabulary outlined in Focus Education's 'geographical knowledge mats'.

Geography: Key Stage 1

Locational Knowledge		Place Knowledge	Human and Physical Geography		Skills and Fieldwork
• name, locate and identify characteristics of the four countries and capital cities of the United Kingdom and its surrounding seas	• name and locate the world's seven continents and five oceans	• understand geographical similarities and differences through studying the human and physical geography of a small area of the United Kingdom, and of a small area in a contrasting non-European country	• identify seasonal and daily weather patterns in the United Kingdom and the location of hot and cold areas of the world in relation to the Equator and the North and South Poles	• use basic geographical vocabulary to refer to: • beach, cliff, coast, forest, hill, mountain, sea, ocean, river, soil, valley, vegetation, season and weather • city, town, village, factory, farm, house, office, port, harbour and shop	• Use world maps, atlases and globes • Use simple compass directions • Use aerial photos, construct simple maps • Undertake simple fieldwork within school locality
Year 1	• Know the names of the four countries that make up the UK and name the three main seas that surround the UK	• Know features of hot and cold places in the world	• Know which is the hottest and coldest season in the UK • Know and recognise main weather symbols • Know the main differences between city, town and village		• Know where the equator, North Pole and South Pole are on a globe • Know which is N, E, S and W on a compass • Know their address, including postcode
Year 2	• Know the names of and locate the seven continents of the world • Know the names of and locate the five oceans of the world • Know the name of and locate the four capital cities of England, Wales, Scotland and Northern Ireland	• Know the main differences between a place in England and that of a small place in a non-European country	• Identify the following physical features: mountain, lake, island, valley, river, cliff, forest and beach • Explain some of the advantages and disadvantages of living in a city or village.		• Know and use the terminologies: left and right; below, next to

Geography: Key Stage 2

Locational Knowledge

	locate the world's countries, using maps to focus on Europe (including the location of Russia) and North and South America, concentrating on their environmental regions, key physical and human characteristics, countries, and major cities	name and locate counties and cities of the United Kingdom, geographical regions and their identifying human and physical characteristics, key topographical features (including hills, mountains, coasts and rivers), and land-use patterns; and understand how some of these aspects have changed over time	identify the position and significance of latitude, longitude, Equator, Northern Hemisphere, Southern Hemisphere, the Tropics of Cancer and Capricorn, Arctic and Antarctic Circle, the Prime/Greenwich Meridian and time zones (including day and night)
Year 3	• Know the names of and locate at least eight European countries	• Know the names of and locate at least eight counties and at least six cities in England	• Know the names of four countries from the southern and four from the northern hemisphere
Year 4	• Know the names of and locate at least eight major capital cities across the world	• Know where the main mountain regions are in the UK • Know, name and locate the main rivers in the UK	• Know where the equator, Tropic of Cancer, Tropic of Capricorn and the Greenwich Meridian are on a world map • Know what is meant by the term 'tropics'
Year 5	• Know the names of a number of European capitals • Know the names of, and locate, a number of South or North American countries		
Year 6			• Know about time zones and work out differences

Geography: Key Stage 2

	Place Knowledge	Human and Physical Geography	
	understand geographical similarities and differences through the study of human and physical geography of a region of the United Kingdom, a region in a European country, and a region within North or South America	*describe and understand key aspects of physical geography, including: climate zones, biomes and vegetation belts, rivers, mountains, volcanoes and earthquakes, and the water cycle*	*describe and understand key aspects of human geography, including types of settlement and land use, economic activity including trade links, and the distribution of natural resources including energy, food, minerals and water*
Year 3	• Know at least five differences between living in the UK and a Mediterranean country	• Know what causes an earthquake • Label the different parts of a volcano	
Year 4		• Know and label the main features of a river • Know the name of and locate a number of the world's longest rivers • Know the names of a number of the world's highest mountains • Explain the features of a water cycle	• Know why most cities are located by a river
Year 5	• Know key differences between living in the UK and in a country in either North or South America	• Know what is meant by biomes and what are the features of a specific biome • Label layers of a rainforest and know what deforestation is	
Year 6		• Know the names of and locate some of the world's deserts	• Know why are industrial areas and ports are important • Know main human and physical differences between developed and third world countries

Geography: Key Stage 2

Geographical skills and fieldwork

	use maps, atlases, globes and digital/computer mapping to locate countries and describe features studied	*use the eight points of a compass, four and six-figure grid references, symbols and key (including the use of Ordnance Survey maps) to build their knowledge of the United Kingdom and the wider world*
Year 3	• Use maps to locate European countries and capitals.	• Know and name the eight points of a compass
Year 4	• Use maps and globes to locate the equator, the Tropics of Cancer and Capricorn and the Greenwich Meridian	• Know how to plan a journey within the UK, using a road map
Year 5	• Know how to use graphs to record features such as temperature or rainfall across the world	
Year 6	• Use Google Earth to locate a country or place of interest and to follow the journey of rivers, etc.	• Know what most of the ordnance survey symbols stand for • Know how to use six-figure grid references

What are the key features of 'knowledge-rich' assessment for history?

Subject	Features
History	❑ At key stage 2, the sticky knowledge takes full account of the national curriculum's main characteristics of: 　❑ Chronology, from the stone age to 1066 　❑ One study beyond 1066 　❑ Ancient civilizations 　❑ Civilizations around 900AD 　❑ Ancient Greece
	❑ There are relatively few assessment statements as these knowledge statements should be what pupils retain for ever. In other words, this knowledge is within their long-term memory and will be retained.
	❑ There is a difference between knowledge which will be retained close to the point of teaching and that which will be retained for ever.
	❑ In effect, sticky knowledge refers to the long-term memory and should not be assessed too close to the point of teaching.
	❑ When considering pupils' improvement in subject specific vocabulary, see the identified historical specific vocabulary outlined in Focus Education's 'historical knowledge mats'.

History: Key Stage 1

	Within living memory	Beyond living memory	Lives of significant people	Local history
	changes within living memory. Where appropriate, these should be used to reveal aspects of change in national life	events beyond living memory that are significant nationally or globally (for example, the Great Fire of London, the first aeroplane flight or events commemorated through festivals or anniversaries)	the lives of significant individuals in the past who have contributed to national and international achievements. Some should be used to compare aspects of life in different periods	significant historical events, people and places in their own locality
Year 1	• Know that the toys their grandparents played with were different to their own • Organise a number of artefacts by age • Know what a number of older objects were used for • Know the main differences between their school days and that of their grandparents		• Name a famous person from the past and explain why they are famous	• Know the name of a famous person, or a famous place, close to where they live
Year 2		• Know about an event or events that happened long ago, even before their grandparents were born • Know what we use today instead of a number of older given artefacts • Know that children's lives today are different to those of children a long time ago	• Know about a famous person from outside the UK and explain why they are famous	• Know how the local area is different to the way it used to be a long time ago • Differentiate between things that were here 100 years ago and things that were not (including buildings, tools, toys, etc.

History: Key Stage 2

CHRONOLOGY (Stone age to 1066)	Beyond 1066	LOCAL STUDY
To include: - *Stone age to Iron age* - *Romans* - *Anglo-Saxons* - *Vikings*	- *An aspect of theme that takes pupils beyond 1066*	- *A local study linked to one of the periods of time studied under chronology; or* - *A local study that could extend beyond 1066*
Year 3 - Know how Britain changed between the beginning of the stone age and the iron age - Know the main differences between the stone, bronze and iron ages - Know what is meant by 'hunter-gatherers'		
Year 4 - Know how Britain changed from the iron age to the end of the Roman occupation - Know how the Roman occupation of Britain helped to advance British society - Know how there was resistance to the Roman occupation and know about Boudica - Know about at least one famous Roman emperor		

History: Key Stage 2

	ANCIENT ANCIENTS (approx. 3000 years ago)	CIVILIZATIONS from 1000 years ago	ANCIENT GREECE
	Cover each of and then choose one to look at in depth: *Ancient Egypt* *Ancient Sumer* *Indus Valley* *Shang Dynasty*	*Choose one of:* *Mayans* *Islamic Civilizations* *Benin Civilization*	*Greek life and influence on the Western world*
Year 3			• Know some of the main characteristics of the Athenians and the Spartans • Know about the influence the gods had on Ancient Greece • Know at least five sports from the Ancient Greek Olympics
Year 4	• Know about, and name, some of the advanced societies that were in the world around 3000 years ago • Know about the key features of either: Ancient Egypt; Ancient Sumer; Indus Valley; or the Shang Dynasty		

History: Key Stage 2

CHRONOLOGY (Stone age to 1066)	Beyond 1066	LOCAL STUDY
- To include: - Stone age to Iron age - Romans - Anglo-Saxons - Vikings	- An aspect of theme that takes pupils beyond 1066	- A local study linked to one of the periods of time studied under chronology; or - A local study that could extend beyond 1066
Year 5 - Know how Britain changed between the end of the Roman occupation and 1066 - Know about how the Anglo-Saxons attempted to bring about law and order into the country - Know that during the Anglo-Saxon period Britain was divided into many kingdoms - Know that the way the kingdoms were divided led to the creation of some of our county boundaries today - Use a time line to show when the Anglo-Saxons were in England		- Know about a period of history that has strong connections to their locality and understand the issues associated with the period. - Know how the lives of wealthy people were different from the lives of poorer people during this time
Year 6 - Know where the Vikings originated from and show this on a map - Know that the Vikings and Anglo-Saxons were often in conflict - Know why the Vikings frequently won battles with the Anglo-Saxons	- Know about a theme in British history which extends beyond 1066 and explain why this was important in relation to British history - Know how to place historical events and people from the past societies and periods in a chronological framework - know how Britain has had a major influence on the world	

History: Key Stage 2

	ANCIENT ANCIENTS (approx. 3000 years ago)	CIVILIZATIONS from 1000 years ago	ANCIENT GREECE
	• *Cover each of and then choose one to look at in depth:* • *Ancient Egypt* • *Ancient Sumer* • *Indus Valley* • *Shang Dynasty*	• *Choose one of:* • *Mayans* • *Islamic Civilizations* • *Benin Civilization*	• *Greek life and influence on the Western world*
Year 5			
Year 6		• Know about the impact that one of the following ancient societies had on the world: the Mayan civilization; the Islamic civilization; or the Benin • Know why they were considered an advanced society in relation to that period of time in Europe	

What are the key features of 'knowledge-rich' assessment for art?

Subject	Features

Art	❑ At key stage 1, the sticky knowledge takes full account of the national curriculum's main characteristics of:
	  ❑ Using materials
	  ❑ Drawing
	  ❑ Use colour, pattern, texture, line, shape, form and space
	  ❑ A study of a range of artists

	❑ At key stage 2, the sticky knowledge takes full account of the national curriculum's main characteristics of:
	  ❑ Using sketch books
	  ❑ Drawing, painting and sculpture
	  ❑ Study of great artists

	❑ There are relatively few assessment statements as these knowledge statements should be what pupils retain for ever. In other words, this knowledge is within their long-term memory and will be retained.
	❑ When considering pupils' improvement in subject specific vocabulary, provide pupils with a vocabulary mat which contains all words used for art for their age group.

Art: Key Stage 1

	Using Materials	Drawing	Use colour, pattern, texture, line, form, space and shape	Range of artists
	use a range of materials creatively to design and make products	*use drawing, painting and sculpture to develop and share their ideas, experiences and imagination*	*develop a wide range of art and design techniques in using colour, pattern, texture, line, shape, form and space*	*Study a range of artists, craft makers and designers*
Year 1	<ul><li>know how to cut, roll and coil materials</li><li>know how to use IT to create a picture</li></ul>	<ul><li>know how to show how people feel in paintings and drawings.</li><li>know how to use pencils to create lines of different thickness in drawings.</li></ul>	<ul><li>know how to create moods in art work</li><li>Know the names of the primary and secondary colours.</li><li>know how to create a repeating pattern in print</li></ul>	<ul><li>describe what can be seen and give an opinion about the work of an artist</li><li>ask questions about a piece of art</li></ul>
Year 2	<ul><li>know how to create a printed piece of art by pressing, rolling, rubbing and stamping</li><li>know how to make a clay pot and know how to join two clay finger pots together</li><li>know how to use different effects within an IT paint package</li></ul>	<ul><li>choose and use three different grades of pencil when drawing</li><li>know how to use charcoal, pencil and pastel to create art</li><li>know how to use a viewfinder to focus on a specific part of an artefact before drawing it</li></ul>	<ul><li>know how to mix paint to create all the secondary colours</li><li>know how to create brown with paint</li><li>know how to create tints with paint by adding white and know how to create tones with paint by adding black</li></ul>	<ul><li>suggest how artists have used colour, pattern and shape</li><li>know how to create a piece of art in response to the work of another artist</li></ul>

Art: Key Stage 2

	Using Sketchbooks	Drawing, painting and sculpture	Study of great artists
	create sketch books to record their observations and use them to review and revisit ideas	*improve their mastery of art and design techniques, including drawing, painting and sculpture with a range of materials (for example, pencil, charcoal, paint, clay)*	*great artists, architects and designers in history*
Year 3	<ul><li>know how to use sketches to produce a final piece of art</li><li>know how to use digital images and combine with other media know how to use IT to create art which includes their own work and that of others</li></ul>	<ul><li>know how to show facial expressions in art.</li><li>know how to use different grades of pencil to shade and to show different tones and textures</li><li>know how to create a background using a wash</li><li>know how to use a range of brushes to create different effects in painting</li></ul>	<ul><li>know how to identify the techniques used by different artists</li><li>know how to compare the work of different artists</li><li>recognise when art is from different cultures</li><li>recognise when art is from different historical periods</li></ul>
Year 4	<ul><li>know how to integrate digital images into artwork.</li><li>Use sketchbooks to help create facial expressions</li><li>use sketchbooks to experiment with different texture</li><li>use photographs to help create reflections</li></ul>	<ul><li>know how to show facial expressions and body language in sketches and paintings</li><li>know how to use marks and lines to show texture in art.</li><li>know how to use line, tone, shape and colour to represent figures and forms in movement and know how to show reflections</li><li>know how to print onto different materials using at least four colours.</li><li>know how to sculpt clay and other mouldable materials.</li></ul>	<ul><li>experiment with the styles used by other artists.</li><li>explain some of the features of art from historical periods.</li><li>know how different artists developed their specific techniques</li></ul>

Art: Key Stage 2

	Using Sketchbooks	Drawing, painting and sculpture	Study of great artists
	- create sketch books to record their observations and use them to review and revisit ideas	- improve their mastery of art and design techniques, including drawing, painting and sculpture with a range of materials (for example, pencil, charcoal, paint, clay)	- great artists, architects and designers in history
Year 5	- experiment by using marks and lines to produce texture - experiment with shading to create mood and feeling - experiment with media to create emotion in art - know how to use images created, scanned and found; altering them where necessary to create art	- know how to use shading to create mood and feeling - know how to organise line, tone, shape and colour to represent figures and forms in movement. - know how to express emotion in art - know how to create an accurate print design following given criteria.	- research the work of an artist and use their work to replicate a style
Year 6	- explain why different tools have been used to create art - explain why chosen specific techniques have been used - know how to use feedback to make amendments and improvement to art - know how to use a range of e-resources to create art	- know how to overprint to create different patterns - know which media to use to create maximum impact - use a full range of pencils, charcoal or pastels when creating a piece of observational art	- explain the style of art used and how it has been influenced by a famous artist - understand what a specific artist is trying to achieve in any given situation - understand why art can be very abstract and what message the artist is trying to convey

What are the key features of 'knowledge-rich' assessment for DT?

Subject	Features

Design Technology	❑ At key stage 1 and 2, the sticky knowledge takes full account of the national curriculum's main characteristics of:
	    ❑ Designing
	    ❑ Making
	    ❑ Evaluating
	    ❑ Using technical knowledge
	    ❑ Food technology

	❑ There are relatively few assessment statements as these knowledge statements should be what pupils retain for ever. In other words, this knowledge is within their long-term memory and will be retained.
	❑ When considering pupils' improvement in subject specific vocabulary, provide pupils with a vocabulary mat which contains all words used for design technology for their age group.

DT: Key Stage 1

	Designing	Making	Evaluating	Technical Knowledge	Food Technology
	Design - purposeful, functional, appealing products for themselves and other users based on design criteria *Design - generate, develop, model and communicate their ideas through talking, drawing, templates, mock-ups and, where appropriate, information and communication technology*	*select from and use a range of tools and equipment to perform practical tasks (for example, cutting, shaping, joining and finishing)* *select from and use a wide range of materials and components, including construction materials, textiles and ingredients, according to their characteristics*	*explore and evaluate a range of existing products evaluate their ideas and products against design criteria*	*build structures, exploring how they can be made stronger, stiffer and more stable* *explore and use mechanisms (for example, levers, sliders, wheels and axles), in their products.*	*use the basic principles of a healthy and varied diet to prepare dishes* *understand where food comes from*
Year 1	• use own ideas to design something and describe how their own idea works • design a product which moves • explain to someone else how they want to make their product and make a simple plan before making	• use own ideas to make something • make a product which moves • choose appropriate resources and tools	• describe how something works • explain what works well and not so well in the model they have made	• make their own model stronger	• cut food safely
Year 2	• think of an idea and plan what to do next • explain why they have chosen specific textiles	• choose tools and materials and explain why they have chosen them • join materials and components in different ways • measure materials to use in a model or structure	• explain what went well with their work	• make a model stronger and more stable • use wheels and axles, when appropriate to do so	• weigh ingredients to use in a recipe • describe the ingredients used when making a dish or cake

© Focus Education (UK) Ltd

DT: Key Stage 2

	Designing	Making	Evaluating	Technical Knowledge	Food Technology
	use research and develop design criteria to inform the design of innovative, functional, appealing products that are fit for purpose, aimed at particular individuals or groups generate, develop, model and communicate their ideas through discussion, annotated sketches, cross-sectional and exploded diagrams, prototypes, pattern pieces and computer-aided design	select from and use a wider range of tools and equipment to perform practical tasks (for example, cutting, shaping, joining and finishing), accurately select from and use a wide range of materials and components, including construction materials, textiles and ingredients, according to their functional properties and aesthetic qualities	investigate and analyse a range of existing products evaluate their ideas and products against their own design criteria and consider the views of others to improve their work understand how key events and individuals in design and technology have helped shape the world	apply their understanding of how to strengthen, stiffen and reinforce more complex structures understand and use mechanical systems in their products (for example, gears, pulleys, cams, levers and linkages) understand and use electrical systems in their products (for example, series circuits incorporating switches, bulbs, buzzers and motors) apply their understanding of computing to program, monitor and control their products.	understand and apply the principles of a healthy and varied diet prepare and cook a variety of predominantly savoury dishes using a range of cooking techniques understand seasonality and know where and how a variety of ingredients are grown, reared, caught and processed
Year 3	• prove that a design meets a set criteria. • design a product and make sure that it looks attractive • choose a material for both its suitability and its appearance	• follow a step-by-step plan, choosing the right equipment and materials • select the most appropriate tools and techniques for a given task • make a product which uses both electrical and mechanical components • work accurately to measure, make cuts and make holes	• explain how to improve a finished model • know why a model has, or has not, been successful	• know how to strengthen a product by stiffening a given part or reinforce a part of the structure • use a simple IT program within the design	• describe how food ingredients come together • weigh out ingredients and follow a given recipe to create a dish • talk about which food is healthy and which food is not • know when food is ready for harvesting
Year 4	• use ideas from other people when designing • produce a plan and explain it • persevere and adapt work when original ideas do not work • communicate ideas in a range of ways, including by sketches and drawings which are annotated	• know which tools to use for a particular task and show knowledge of handling the tool • know which material is likely to give the best outcome • measure accurately	• evaluate and suggest improvements for design • evaluate products for both their purpose and appearance • explain how the original design has been improved • present a product in an interesting way	• links scientific knowledge by using lights, switches or buzzers • use electrical systems to enhance the quality of the product • use IT, where appropriate, to add to the quality of the product	• know how to be both hygienic and safe when using food • bring a creative element to the food product being designed

DT: Key Stage 2

	Designing	Making	Evaluating	Technical Knowledge	Food Technology
	use research and develop design criteria to inform the design of innovative, functional, appealing products that are fit for purpose, aimed at particular individuals or groups *generate, develop, model and communicate their ideas through discussion, annotated sketches, cross-sectional and exploded diagrams, prototypes, pattern pieces and computer-aided design*	*select from and use a wider range of tools and equipment to perform practical tasks (for example, cutting, shaping, joining and finishing), accurately select from and use a wide range of materials and components, including construction materials, textiles and ingredients, according to their functional properties and aesthetic qualities*	*investigate and analyse a range of existing products evaluate their ideas and products against their own design criteria and consider the views of others to improve their work understand how key events and individuals in design and technology have helped shape the world*	*apply their understanding of how to strengthen, stiffen and reinforce more complex structures* *understand and use mechanical systems in their products (for example, gears, pulleys, cams, levers and linkages)* *understand and use electrical systems in their products (for example, series circuits incorporating switches, bulbs, buzzers and motors)* *apply their understanding of computing to program, monitor and control their products.*	*understand and apply the principles of a healthy and varied diet* *prepare and cook a variety of predominantly savoury dishes using a range of cooking techniques* *understand seasonality and know where and how a variety of ingredients are grown, reared, caught and processed*
Year 5	<ul><li>come up with a range of ideas after collecting information from different sources</li><li>produce a detailed, step-by-step plan</li><li>explain how a product will appeal to a specific audience</li><li>design a product that requires pulleys or gears</li></ul>	<ul><li>use a range of tools and equipment competently</li><li>make a prototype before making a final version</li><li>make a product that relies on pulleys or gears</li></ul>	<ul><li>suggest alternative plans; outlining the positive features and draw backs</li><li>evaluate appearance and function against original criteria</li></ul>	<ul><li>links scientific knowledge to design by using pulleys or gears</li><li>uses more complex IT program to help enhance the quality of the product produced</li></ul>	<ul><li>be both hygienic and safe in the kitchen</li><li>know how to prepare a meal by collecting the ingredients in the first place</li><li>know which season various foods are available for harvesting</li></ul>
Year 6	<ul><li>use market research to inform plans and ideas.</li><li>follow and refine original plans</li><li>justify planning in a convincing way</li><li>show that culture and society is considered in plans and designs</li></ul>	<ul><li>know which tool to use for a specific practical task</li><li>know how to use any tool correctly and safely</li><li>know what each tool is used for</li><li>explain why a specific tool is best for a specific action</li></ul>	<ul><li>know how to test and evaluate designed products</li><li>explain how products should be stored and give reasons</li><li>evaluate product against clear criteria</li></ul>	<ul><li>use electrical systems correctly and accurately to enhance a given product</li><li>know which IT product would further enhance a specific product</li><li>use knowledge to improve a made product by strengthening, stiffening or reinforcing</li></ul>	<ul><li>explain how food ingredients should be stored and give reasons</li><li>work within a budget to create a meal</li><li>understand the difference between a savoury and sweet dish</li></ul>

What are the key features of 'knowledge-rich' assessment for Music?

Subject	Features
Music	❑ At key stage 1, the sticky knowledge takes full account of the national curriculum's main characteristics of: 　❑ Singing 　❑ Playing an instrument 　❑ Listening and Appreciating 　❑ Creating own music
	❑ At key stage 2, the sticky knowledge takes full account of the national curriculum's main characteristics of: 　❑ Performing 　❑ Composing 　❑ Listening 　❑ Use and understand 　❑ Appreciate 　❑ History of Music
	❑ There are relatively few assessment statements as these knowledge statements should be what pupils retain for ever. In other words, this knowledge is within their long-term memory and will be retained.
	❑ When considering pupils' improvement in subject specific vocabulary, provide pupils with a vocabulary mat which contains all words used for music for their age group.

Music: Key Stage 1

	Singing	Playing an instrument	Listening and appreciate	Create own music
	Pupils should be taught to use their voices expressively and creatively by singing songs and speaking chants and rhymes	*Pupils should be taught to play tuned and untuned instruments musically*	*Pupils should be taught to listen with concentration and understanding to a range of high-quality live and recorded music*	*Pupils should be taught to experiment with, create, select and combine sounds using the inter-related dimensions of music*
Year 1	<ul><li>make different sounds with voice and with instruments</li><li>follow instructions about when to play and sing</li></ul>	<ul><li>use instruments to perform and choose sounds to represent different things</li></ul>	<ul><li>say whether they like or dislike a piece of music</li></ul>	<ul><li>clap and repeat short rhythmic and melodic patterns</li><li>make a sequence of sounds and respond to different moods in music</li></ul>
Year 2	<ul><li>sing or clap increasing and decreasing tempo</li><li>perform simple patterns and accompaniments keeping a steady pulse</li></ul>	<ul><li>play simple rhythmic patterns on an instrument</li></ul>	<ul><li>make connections between notations and musical sounds</li></ul>	<ul><li>order sounds to create a beginning, middle and an end</li><li>create music in response to different starting points</li></ul>

Music: Key Stage 2

	Performing	Compose	Listen
	play and perform in solo and ensemble contexts, using their voices and playing musical instruments with increasing accuracy, fluency, control and expression	*improvise and compose music for a range of purposes using the inter-related dimensions of music*	*listen with attention to detail and recall sounds with increasing aural memory*
Year 3	• play clear notes on instruments and use different elements in composition	• combine different sounds to create a specific mood or feeling	• listen carefully and recognise high and low phrases
Year 4	• sing songs from memory with accurate pitch	• use notation to record compositions in a small group or individually	• explain why silence is often needed in music and explain what effect it has
Year 5	• maintain own part whilst others are performing their part	• compose music which meets specific criteria • choose the most appropriate tempo for a piece of music	• repeat a phrase from the music after listening intently.
Year 6	• sing in harmony confidently and accurately • perform parts from memory • take the lead in a performance	• use a variety of different musical devices in composition (including melody, rhythms and chords).	• accurately recall a part of the music listened to

Music: Key Stage 2

	Use and understand	Appreciate	History of music
	use and understand staff and other musical notations	*appreciate and understand a wide range of high-quality live and recorded music drawn from different traditions and from great composers and musicians*	*develop an understanding of the history of music*
Year 3	<ul><li>create repeated patterns with different instruments</li><li>improve my work; explaining how it has been improved</li></ul>	<ul><li>use musical words to describe a piece of music and compositions</li><li>use musical words to describe what they like and do not like about a piece of music</li></ul>	<ul><li>recognise the work of at least one famous composer</li></ul>
Year 4	<ul><li>use notation to record and interpret sequences of pitches</li></ul>	<ul><li>identify and describe the different purposes of music</li></ul>	<ul><li>begin to identify the style of work of Beethoven, Mozart and Elgar</li></ul>
Year 5	<ul><li>use music diary to record aspects of the composition process</li></ul>	<ul><li>describe, compare and evaluate music using musical vocabulary</li><li>explain why they think music is successful or unsuccessful</li></ul>	<ul><li>contrast the work of a famous composer with another and explain preferences</li></ul>
Year 6	<ul><li>analyse features within different pieces of music</li></ul>	<ul><li>evaluate how the venue, occasion and purpose affects the way a piece of music is created</li></ul>	<ul><li>compare and contrast the impact that different composers from different times have had on people of that time</li></ul>

What are the key features of 'knowledge-rich' assessment for Computing?

Subject	Features

Computing	❑ At key stage 1, the sticky knowledge takes full account of the national curriculum's main characteristics of:
	  ❑ Algorithms
	  ❑ Creating Programs
	  ❑ Reasoning
	  ❑ Using Technology
	  ❑ Uses of IT beyond school
	  ❑ Being Safe

	❑ At key stage 2, the sticky knowledge takes full account of the national curriculum's main characteristics of:
	  ❑ Creating Programs
	  ❑ Developing Programs
	  ❑ Reasoning
	  ❑ Networks
	  ❑ Search Engines
	  ❑ Using Programs
	  ❑ Being Safe

	❑ There are relatively few assessment statements as these knowledge statements should be what pupils retain for ever. In other words, this knowledge is within their long-term memory and will be retained.
	❑ When considering pupils' improvement in subject specific vocabulary, provide pupils with a vocabulary mat which contains all words used for computing for their age group.

Computing: Key Stage 1

	Algorithms	Create programs	Reasoning
	Pupils should be taught to understand what algorithms are; how they are implemented as programs on digital devices; and that programs execute by following precise and unambiguous instructions	*Pupils should be taught to create and debug simple programs*	*Pupils should be taught to use logical reasoning to predict the behaviour of simple programs*
Year 1	• create a series of instructions and plan a journey for a programmable toy	• create, store and retrieve digital content	
Year 2	• understand that algorithms are used on digital devices	• write a simple program and test it	• predict what the outcome of a simple program will be (logical reasoning).

Computing: Key Stage 1

	Using technology	Uses of IT beyond school	Safe use
	Pupils should be taught to use technology purposefully to create, organise, store, manipulate and retrieve digital	*Pupils should be taught to recognise common uses of information technology beyond school*	*Pupils should be taught to use technology safely and respectfully, keeping personal information private; identify where to go for help and support when they have concerns about content or contact on the internet or other online technologies*
Year 1	<ul><li>use a website and a camera</li><li>record sound and play back</li></ul>	<ul><li>talk about some of the IT uses in their own home</li></ul>	<ul><li>use technology safely</li><li>keep personal information private</li></ul>
Year 2	<ul><li>understand that programs require precise instructions</li><li>organise, retrieve and manipulate digital content</li></ul>	<ul><li>know how technology is used in school and outside of school</li></ul>	<ul><li>know where to go for help if concerned.</li></ul>

Computing: Key Stage 2

	Create programs	Develop programs	Reasoning	Networks
	Pupils should be taught to design, write and debug programs that accomplish specific goals, including controlling or simulating physical systems; solve problems by decomposing them into smaller parts	*Pupils should be taught to use sequence, selection, and repetition in programs; work with variables and various forms of input and output*	*Pupils should be taught to use logical reasoning to explain how some simple algorithms work and to detect and correct errors in algorithms and programs*	*Pupils should be taught to understand computer networks including the internet; how they can provide multiple services, such as the world wide web; and the opportunities they offer for communication and collaboration*
Year 3	• write programs that accomplish specific goals	• design a sequence of instructions, including directional instructions	• discern when it is best to use technology and where it adds little or no value	• navigate the web to complete simple searches
Year 4	• give an 'on-screen' robot specific instructions that takes them from A to B	• experiment with variables to control models	• make an accurate prediction and explain why they believe something will happen (linked to programming)	• know how to search for specific information and know which information is useful and which is not
Year 5	• use technology to control an external device	• develop a program that has specific variables identified	• analyse and evaluate information reaching a conclusion that helps with future developments	
Year 6	• write a program that combines more than one attribute	• develop a sequenced program that has repetition and variables identified	• design algorithms that use repetition and 2-way selection	

Computing: Key Stage 2

	Search engines	Using programs	Safe use
	Pupils should be taught to use search technologies effectively, appreciate how results are selected and ranked, and be discerning in evaluating digital content	*Pupils should be taught to select, use and combine a variety of software (including internet services) on a range of digital devices to design and create a range of programs, systems and content that accomplish given goals, including collecting, analysing, evaluating and presenting data and information*	*Pupils should be taught to use technology safely, respectfully and responsibly; recognise acceptable/unacceptable behaviour; identify a range of ways to report concerns about content and contact*
Year 3	<ul><li>use a range of software for similar purposes</li><li>collect and present information</li></ul>	<ul><li>understand what computer networks do and how they provide multiple services</li></ul>	<ul><li>use technology respectfully and responsibly</li><li>Know different ways they can get help if concerned</li></ul>
Year 4	<ul><li>select and use software to accomplish given goals</li></ul>	<ul><li>produce and upload a podcast</li></ul>	<ul><li>recognise acceptable and unacceptable behaviour using technology</li></ul>
Year 5	<ul><li>understand how search results are selected and ranked</li></ul>	<ul><li>combine sequences of instructions and procedures to turn devices on and off</li></ul>	<ul><li>understand that they have to make choices when using technology and that not everything is true and/or safe</li></ul>
Year 6	<ul><li>be aware that some search engines may provide misleading information</li></ul>	<ul><li>present the data collected in a way that makes it easy for others to understand</li></ul>	<ul><li>Be increasingly aware of the potential dangers in using aspects of IT and know when to alert someone if feeling uncomfortable</li></ul>

What are the key features of 'knowledge-rich' assessment for Physical Education?

Subject	Features
Physical Education	❏ At key stage 1, the sticky knowledge takes full account of the national curriculum's main characteristics of: 　❏ Gymnastics 　❏ Basic Movement and Team Games 　❏ Dance
	❏ At key stage 2, the sticky knowledge takes full account of the national curriculum's main characteristics of: 　❏ Athletics 　❏ Gymnastics 　❏ Competitive Games 　❏ Outdoor Adventure 　❏ Dance 　❏ Swimming 　❏ Evaluating
	❏ There are relatively few assessment statements as these knowledge statements should be what pupils retain for ever. In other words, this knowledge is within their long-term memory and will be retained.
	❏ When considering pupils' improvement in subject specific vocabulary, provide pupils with a vocabulary mat which contains all words used for PE for their age group.

Physical Education: Key Stage 1

	Gymnastic Movements	Basic movements and Team Games	Dance
	developing balance, agility and co-ordination, and begin to apply these in a range of activities	*master basic movements including running, jumping, throwing and catching, as well as participate in team games, developing simple tactics for attacking and defending*	*perform dances using simple movement patterns*
Year 1	<ul><li>make body curled, tense, stretched and relaxed</li><li>control body when travelling and balancing</li><li>copy sequences and repeat them</li><li>roll, curl, travel and balance in different ways</li></ul>	<ul><li>throw underarm</li><li>throw and kick in different ways</li></ul>	<ul><li>perform own dance moves</li><li>copy or make up a short dance</li><li>move safely in a space</li></ul>
Year 2	<ul><li>plan and perform a sequence of movements</li><li>improve sequence based on feedback</li><li>think of more than one way to create a sequence which follows some 'rules'</li></ul>	<ul><li>use hitting, kicking and/or rolling in a game</li><li>decide the best space to be in during a game</li><li>use a tactic in a game</li><li>follow rules</li></ul>	<ul><li>change rhythm, speed, level and direction in dance</li><li>make a sequence by linking sections together</li><li>use dance to show a mood or feeling</li></ul>

Physical Education: Key Stage 2

	Athletics	Competitive Games	Gymnastics
	use running, jumping, throwing and catching in isolation and in combination	*play competitive games, modified where appropriate (for example, badminton, basketball, cricket, football, hockey, netball, rounders and tennis), and apply basic principles suitable for attacking and defending*	*develop flexibility, strength, technique, control and balance (for example, through athletics and gymnastics)*
Year 3	<ul><li>run at fast, medium and slow speeds; changing speed and direction</li><li>take part in a relay, remembering when to run and what to do</li></ul>	<ul><li>be aware of space and use it to support team-mates and to cause problems for the opposition</li><li>know and use rules fairly</li></ul>	<ul><li>adapt sequences to suit different types of apparatus and criteria</li><li>explain how strength and suppleness affect performance</li></ul>
Year 4	<ul><li>sprint over a short distance and show stamina when running over a long distance</li><li>jump in different ways</li><li>throw in different ways and hit a target, when needed</li></ul>	<ul><li>throw and catch accurately with one hand</li><li>hit a ball accurately with control</li><li>vary tactics and adapt skills depending on what is happening in a game</li></ul>	<ul><li>move in a controlled way</li><li>include change of speed and direction in a sequence</li><li>work with a partner to create, repeat and improve a sequence with at least three phases</li></ul>
Year 5	<ul><li>controlled when taking off and landing</li><li>throw with increasing accuracy</li><li>combine running and jumping</li></ul>	<ul><li>gain possession by working a team and pass in different ways</li><li>choose a specific tactic for defending and attacking</li><li>use a number of techniques to pass, dribble and shoot</li></ul>	<ul><li>make complex extended sequences</li><li>combine action, balance and shape</li><li>perform consistently to different audiences</li></ul>
Year 6	<ul><li>demonstrate stamina and increase strength</li></ul>	<ul><li>agree and explain rules to others</li><li>work as a team and communicate a plan</li><li>lead others in a game situation when the need arises</li></ul>	<ul><li>combine own work with that of others</li><li>sequences to specific timings</li></ul>

Physical Education: Key Stage 2

	Dance	Outdoor and Adventurous Activity	Evaluate
	perform dances using a range of movement patterns	*take part in outdoor and adventurous activity challenges both individually and within a team*	*compare their performances with previous ones and demonstrate improvement to achieve their personal best*
Year 3	<ul><li>improvise freely and translate ideas from a stimulus into movement</li><li>share and create phrases with a partner and small group</li><li>remember and repeat dance perform phrases</li></ul>	<ul><li>follow a map in a familiar context</li><li>use clues to follow a route</li><li>follow a route safely</li></ul>	<ul><li>compare and contrast gymnastic sequences</li><li>recognise own improvement in ball games</li></ul>
Year 4	<ul><li>take the lead when working with a partner or group</li><li>use dance to communicate an idea</li></ul>	<ul><li>follow a map in a (more demanding) familiar context</li><li>follow a route within a time limit</li></ul>	<ul><li>provide support and advice to others in gymnastics and dance</li><li>be prepared to listen to the ideas of others</li></ul>
Year 5	<ul><li>compose own dances in a creative way</li><li>perform dance to an accompaniment</li><li>dance shows clarity, fluency, accuracy and consistency</li></ul>	<ul><li>follow a map into an unknown location</li><li>use clues and a compass to navigate a route</li><li>change route to overcome a problem</li><li>use new information to change route</li></ul>	<ul><li>pick up on something a partner does well and also on something that can be improved</li><li>know why own performance was better or not as good as their last</li></ul>
Year 6	<ul><li>develop sequences in a specific style</li><li>choose own music and style</li></ul>	<ul><li>plan a route and a series of clues for someone else</li><li>plan with others, taking account of safety and danger</li></ul>	<ul><li>know which sports they are good at and find out how to improve further</li></ul>

What are the key features of 'knowledge-rich' assessment for Foreign Languages?

Subject	Features

Foreign Languages	❏ At key stage 2, the sticky knowledge takes full account of the national curriculum's main characteristics of:
	  ❏ Speaking
	  ❏ Reading
	  ❏ Writing

	❏ There are relatively few assessment statements as these knowledge statements should be what pupils retain for ever. In other words, this knowledge is within their long-term memory and will be retained.
	❏ When considering pupils' improvement in subject specific vocabulary, provide pupils with a vocabulary mat which contains all words used for Foreign Language for their age group.

Foreign Language: Key Stage 2

	Speaking	Reading	Writing
	speak in sentences, using familiar vocabulary, phrases and basic language structures	*develop accurate pronunciation and intonation so that others understand when they are reading aloud or using familiar words and phrases*	*broaden their vocabulary and develop their ability to understand new words that are introduced into familiar written material, including through using a dictionary*
Year 3/4	• name and describe people, a place and an object • have a short conversation, saying 3 to 4 things • give response using a short phrase • start to speak, using a full sentence	• read and understand a short passage using familiar language • explain the main points in a short passage • read a passage independently • use a bilingual dictionary or glossary to look up new words	• write phrases from memory • write 2-3 short sentences on a familiar topic • write what they like/dislike about a familiar topic
Year 5/6	• hold a simple conversation with at least 4 exchanges • use knowledge of grammar to speak correctly	• understand a short story or factual text and note the main points • use the context to work out unfamiliar words	• write a paragraph of 4-5 sentences • substitute words and phrases

Appendices

The following pages provides you with a different way of setting out the sticky knowledge for science, geography and history

Sticky Knowledge: Science

Year 1
Science Knowledge
☐ Know and name a variety of common wild and garden plants
☐ Know and name the petals, stem, leaves and root of a plant
☐ Know and name the roots, trunk, branches and leaves of a tree
☐ Know how to classify a range of animals by amphibian, reptile, mammal, fish and birds
☐ Know and classify animals by what they eat (carnivore, herbivore and omnivore)
☐ Know how to sort by living and non living things
☐ Know the name of parts of the human body that can be seen
☐ Know the name of the materials an object is made from
☐ Know about the properties of everyday materials
☐ Name the seasons and know about the type of weather in each season

Sticky Knowledge: Science

Year 2
Science Knowledge
❑ Classify things by living, dead or never lived
❑ Know how a specific habitat provides for the basic needs of things living there (plants and animals).
❑ Match living things to their habitat
❑ Name some different sources of food for animals
❑ Know about and explain a simple food chain
❑ Know and explain how seeds and bulbs grow into plants
❑ Know what plants need in order to grow and stay healthy (water, light and suitable temperature)
❑ Know the basic stages in a life cycle for animals, including humans
❑ Know why exercise, a balanced diet and good hygiene are important for humans
❑ Know why a material might or might not be used for a specific job
❑ Know how materials can be changed by squashing, bending, twisting and stretching

Sticky Knowledge: Science

Year 3

Science Knowledge

☐ Know the function of different parts of flowing plants and trees	☐ Know what dark is the absence of light
☐ Know how water is transported within plants	☐ Know that light is needed in order to see and is reflected from a surface
☐ Know the plant life cycle, especially the importance of flowers	☐ Know and demonstrate how a shadow is formed and explain how a shadow changes shape
☐ Know about the importance of a nutritious, balanced diet	☐ Know about the danger of direct sunlight and describe how to keep protected
☐ Know how nutrients, water and oxygen are transported within animals and humans	☐ Know about and describe how objects move on different surfaces
☐ Know about the skeletal and muscular system of a human	☐ Know how a simple pulley works and use making lifting an object simpler
☐ Compare and group rocks based on their appearance and physical properties, giving a reason	☐ Know how some forces require contact and some do not, giving examples
☐ Know how soil is made and fossils formed	☐ Know about and explain how objects attract and repel in relation to objects and other magnets
☐ Know about and explain the difference between sedimentary, metamorphic and igneous rock	☐ Predict whether magnets will attract or repel and give a reason

Sticky Knowledge: Science

Year 4

Science Knowledge

☐	Use classification keys to group, identify and name living things	☐	Know how sound is made associating some of them with vibrating
☐	Know how changes to an environment could endanger living things	☐	Know how sound travels from a source to our ears
☐	Identify and name the parts of the human digestive system	☐	Know the correlation between pitch and the object producing a sound
☐	Know the functions of the organs in the human digestive system	☐	Know the correlation between the volume of a sound and the strength of the vibrations that produced it
☐	Identify and know the different types of teeth that humans have	☐	Know what happens to a sound as it travels away from its source
☐	Know the functions of different human teeth	☐	Identify and name appliances that require electricity to function
☐	Use and construct food chains to identify producers, predators and prey	☐	Construct a series circuit
☐	Group materials based on their state of matter (solid, liquid, gas	☐	Identify and name the components in a series circuit (including cells, wires, bulbs, switches and buzzers)
☐	Know about and explore how some materials can change state	☐	Predict and test whether a lamp will light within a circuit
☐	Know the temperature at which materials change state	☐	Know the function of a switch in a circuit
☐	Know the part played by evaporation and condensation in the water cycle	☐	Know the difference between a conductor and an insulator; giving examples of each

Sticky Knowledge: Science

Year 5

Science Knowledge

❑ Know the life cycle of different living things, e.g. mammal, amphibian, insect bird	❑ Know and can demonstrate that some changes are reversible and some are not
❑ Know the differences between different life cycles	❑ Know how some changes result in the formation of a new material and that this is usually irreversible
❑ Know the process of reproduction in plants	❑ Know about and explain the movement of the Earth and other planets relative to the Sun
❑ Know the process of reproduction in animals	❑ Know about and explain the movement of the Moon relative to the Earth
❑ Create a timeline to indicate stages of growth in humans	❑ Know and demonstrate how night and day are created
❑ Compare and group materials based on their properties (e.g. hardness, solubility, transparency, conductivity, (electrical & thermal), and response to magnets	❑ Describe the Sun, Earth and Moon (using the term spherical).
	❑ Know what gravity is and its impact on our lives
❑ Know how a material dissolves to form a solution; explaining the process of dissolving	❑ Identify and know the effect of air and water resistance
❑ Know and show how to recover a substance from a solution	❑ Identify and know the effect of friction
❑ Know and demonstrate how some materials can be separated (e.g. through filtering, sieving and evaporating)	❑ Explain how levers, pulleys and gears allow a smaller force to have a greater effect

Sticky Knowledge: Science

Year 6

Science Knowledge

☐ Classify living things into broad groups according to observable characteristics and based on similarities and differences	☐ Know how animals and plants are adapted to suit their environment
☐ Know how living things have been classified	☐ Link adaptation over time to evolution
☐ Give reasons for classifying plants and animals in a specific way	☐ Know about evolution and can explain what it is
☐ Identify and name the main parts of the human circulatory system	☐ Know how light travels
☐ Know the function of the heart, blood vessels and blood	☐ Know and demonstrate how we see objects
☐ Know the impact of diet, exercise, drugs and life style on health	☐ Know why shadows have the same shape as the object that casts them
☐ Know the ways in which nutrients and water are transported in animals, including humans	☐ Know how simple optical instruments work, e.g. periscope, telescope, binoculars, mirror, magnifying glass etc
☐ Know how the Earth and living things have changed over time	☐ Compare and give reasons for why components work and do not work in a circuit
☐ Know how fossils can be used to find out about the past	☐ Draw circuit diagrams using correct symbols
☐ Know about reproduction and offspring (recognising that offspring normally vary and are not identical to their parents)	☐ Know how the number and voltage of cells in a circuit links to the brightness of a lamp or the volume of a buzzer

Sticky Knowledge: Science

Year 6

Working Scientifically

❑	Know which type of investigation is needed to suit particular scientific enquiry, e.g., looking at the relationship between pulse and exercise	❑	Use a range of written methods to report findings, including focusing on the planning, doing and evaluating phases
❑	Set up a fair test when needed, e.g., does light travel in straight lines?	❑	Clear about what has been found out from their enquiry and can relate this to others in the class
❑	Know how to set up an enquiry based investigation, e.g., what is the relationship between oxygen and blood	❑	Explanations set out clearly why something has happened and its possible impact on other things
❑	Know what the variables are in a given enquiry and can isolate each one when investigating	❑	Aware of the need to support conclusions with evidence
❑	Justify which variable has been isolated in scientific investigation	❑	Keep an on-going record of new scientific words that they have come across for the first time and use these regularly in future scientific write ups
❑	Use all measurements as set out in Year 6 mathematics (measurement), this includes capacity, mass, ratio and proportion	❑	Use diagrams, as and when necessary, to support writing and be confident enough to present findings orally in front of the class
❑	Able to record data and present them in a range of ways including, diagrams, labels, classification keys, tables, scatter graphs and bar and line graphs	❑	Able to give an example of something they have focused on when supporting a scientific theory, e.g., classifying vertebrate and invertebrate creatures or why certain creatures choose their unique habitats
❑	Make accurate predictions based on information gleaned from their investigations and create new investigations as a result	❑	Frequently carry out research when investigating a scientific principle or theory
❑	Able to present information related to scientific enquiries in a range of ways including using IT such as power-point, animoto and iMovie		

Sticky Knowledge: Geography

Year 1	Year 2
☐ Know the names of the four countries that make up the UK and name the three main seas that surround the UK	☐ Know the names of and locate the seven continents of the world
☐ Know where the equator, North Pole and South Pole are on a globe	☐ Know the names of and locate the five oceans of the world
☐ Know which is N, E, S and W on a compass	☐ Know the name of and locate the four capital cities of England, Wales, Scotland and Northern Ireland
☐ Know features of hot and cold places in the world	☐ Identify the following physical features: mountain; lake; island: valley: river; cliff; forest and beach
☐ Know which is the hottest and coldest season in the UK	☐ Know the main differences between a place in England and that of a small place in a non-European country
☐ Know and recognise main weather symbols	☐ Know and use the terminologies: left and right; below and next to
☐ Know the main differences between city, town and village	☐ Explain some of the advantages and disadvantages of living in a city or village.
☐ Know their address, including postcode	

Sticky Knowledge: Geography

Year 3	Year 4
❏ Know the names of, and locate, at least eight European countries	❏ Know where the equator, tropic of Cancer, Tropic of Capricorn and the Greenwich meridian are on a world map
❏ Use maps to locate European countries and capitals.	
❏ Know the names of, and locate, at least eight counties and at least six cities in England	❏ Know what is meant by the term 'topics'
❏ Know the names of four countries from the southern and four from the northern hemisphere	❏ Know and label the main features of a river
❏ Know at least five differences between living in the UK and a Mediterranean country	❏ Know why most cities are located by a river
❏ Know what causes an earthquake	❏ Know the name of, and locate, a number of the world's longest rivers
❏ Label the different parts of a volcano	❏ Know the names of a number of the world's highest mountains
❏ Know how to plan a journey within the UK, using a road map	❏ Explain the features of a water cycle

Sticky Knowledge: Geography

Year 5	Year 6
❏ Know the names of a number of European capitals	❏ Know what most of the ordnance survey symbols stand for
❏ Know the names of, and locate, a number of South or North American countries	❏ Know how to use six-figure grid references
❏ Label layers of a rainforest	❏ Know why are industrial areas and ports are important
❏ Know what deforestation means	❏ Know the main human and physical differences between developed and third world countries
❏ Know what is meant by biomes and what are the features of a specific biome	❏ Know about time zones and work out differences
❏ Know how to use graphs to record features such as temperature or rainfall across the world	❏ Know the names of and locate some of the world's deserts
	❏ Use Google Earth to locate a country or place of interest and to follow the journey of rivers, etc.

Sticky Knowledge: History

Year 1	Year 2
❏ Know that the toys their grandparents played with were different to their own	❏ Know about an event or events that happened long ago, even before their grandparents were born
❏ Organise a number of artefacts by age	❏ Know what we use today instead of a number of older given artefacts
❏ Know what a number of older objects were used for	❏ Know about a famous person from outside the UK and explain why they are famous
❏ Know the main differences between their school days and that of their grandparents	❏ Know that children's lives today are different to those of children a long time ago
❏ Name a famous person from the past and explain why they are famous	❏ Know how the local area is different to the way it used to be a long time ago
❏ Know the name of a famous person, or a famous place, close to where they live	❏ Differentiate between things that were here 100 years ago and things that were not (including buildings, tools, toys, etc.

Sticky Knowledge: History

Year 3	Year 4
❏ Know how Britain changed between the beginning of the stone age and the iron age	❏ Know how Britain changed from the iron age to the end of the Roman occupation
❏ Know the main differences between the stone, bronze and iron ages	❏ Know how the Roman occupation of Britain helped to advance British society
❏ Know what is meant by 'hunter-gatherers	❏ Know how there was resistance to the Roman occupation and know about Boudica
❏ Know some of the main characteristics of the Athenians and the Spartans	❏ Know about at least one famous Roman emperor
❏ Know about the influence the Gods had on Ancient Greece	❏ Know about, and name, some of the advanced societies that were in the world about 3000 years ago
❏ Know at least five sports competed in the Ancient Greek Olympics	❏ Know about the key features of either: Ancient Egypt; Ancient Sumer; Indus Valley; or, the Shang Dynasty

Sticky Knowledge: History

Year 5	Year 6
❏ Know how Britain changed between the end of the Roman occupation and 1066	❏ Know about the impact that one of the following ancient societies had on the world: the Mayan civilization; the Islamic civilization; or, the Benin
❏ Know about how the Anglo-Saxons attempted to bring about law and order into the country	❏ Know where the Vikings originated from and show this on a map
❏ Know that during the Anglo-Saxon period Britain was divided into many kingdoms	❏ Know that the Vikings and Anglo-Saxons were often in conflict
❏ Know that the way the kingdoms were divided led to the creation of some of our county boundaries today	❏ Know why the Vikings frequently won battles with the Anglo-Saxons
❏ Know how the lives of wealthy people were different from the lives of poorer people	❏ Know how to place features of historical events and people from the past societies and periods in a chronological framework
❏ Use a time line to show when the Anglo-Saxons were in England	❏ know how Britain has had a major influence on the world

Are you looking to publish your own work?

Focus Education is an independent publisher looking to work with authors of teacher resources in primary schools. With over 25 years experience and an excellent reputation in the primary education market, we can publish and retail your work providing a full wrap around service from order to dispatch.

Advantages of publishing with Focus Education:

- Quick Turnaround

- No unnecessary red tape or administration

- Full editing, formatting & design process

- Competitive royalty rates per sale

- Full order, sale and dispatch service

For more information, please email *claire@focus-education.co.uk*

What do you think?

We love to hear your feedback on our products and services

 Tweet Us

@clivedaviesobe

@focuseducation1